NATIONAL TESTS practice papers

FOR THE YEAR 2004

English
Levels 2–5

practice
papers

AGE
10–11
Key Stage 2

Ray Barker

Christine Moorcroft

Acknowledgements

The authors and publisher would like to thank the copyright owners of the following for permission to reproduce material in this book:

'The Postman' by Jon Stallworthy, from *Root and Branch*, Chatto & Windus
The Wool-Pack by Cynthia Harnett, Methuen 1951, Puffin Books 1961
Postage Stamps by L N and M Williams, Puffin Books

Every effort has been made to trace and acknowledge ownership of copyright material but if any have been inadvertently overlooked, the publisher will be pleased to make the necessary alterations at the first opportunity.

First published 2003
exclusively for WHSmith by
Hodder & Stoughton Educational,
a division of Hodder Headline Ltd
338 Euston Road
London NW1 3BH

Text and illustrations © Hodder & Stoughton Educational 2003

All rights reserved. No part of this publication may be reproduced or transmitted in any form or by any means, electronic or mechanical, including photocopying, recording or any information storage and retrieval system, without permission in writing from the publisher.

A CIP record for this book is available from the British Library.

Authors: Christine Moorcroft and Ray Barker
Series editor: Louis Fidge
Illustrations: Willie Ryan

ISBN 0 340 81377 6

Impression 5 4 3 2 1
           2004 2003

Printed and bound by Hobbs The Printers, Totton, Hampshire

> NOTE: The tests, questions and advice in this book are not reproductions of the official test materials sent to schools. The official testing process is supported by guidance and training for teachers in setting and marking tests and interpreting the results. The results achieved in the tests in this book may not be the same as those achieved in the official tests.

Contents

Introduction — v
The National Tests: A Summary — v
How to use this book — vii
Insights from previous tests — viii
Setting the tests — ix
Advice to give to your child — x

Reading Test — 1
Reading Test Booklet — 1
Reading Test Questions — 7

Writing Test — 17
Writing Test: Information — 17
Writing Test: Story — 21

Spelling Test — 25

Answers — 27
Reading Test — 27
Writing Test — 31
Spelling Test — 35

National Curriculum Levels — 37

Introduction

The National Tests: A Summary

What are the National Tests?

Children who attend state schools in England and Wales sit National Tests (also known as SATs, Standard Assessment Tasks) at the ages of 7, 11 and 14, usually at the beginning of May. They may also sit optional tests in the intervening years – many schools have chosen to adopt these tests. The test results are accompanied by an assessment by the child's teacher (at Key Stage 3 this also covers non-tested subjects such as History or Geography).

The results are used by the school to assess each child's level of knowledge and progress in English and Maths at Key Stage 1 and English, Maths and Science at Key Stages 2 and 3. They also provide useful guidance for the child's next teacher when he or she is planning the year's work.

The educational calendar for children aged 5–14 is structured as follows:

Key Stage	Year	Age by end of year	National Test
1 (KS1)	1	6	
	2	7	KEY STAGE 1
2 (KS2)	3	8	Optional Year 3
	4	9	Optional Year 4
	5	10	Optional Year 5
	6	11	KEY STAGE 2
3 (KS3)	7	12	Optional Year 7
	8	13	Optional Year 8
	9	14	KEY STAGE 3

Timetable

The Key Stage 1 National Tests are carried out in **May**. They often form part of your child's normal school day, as they are generally practical and teacher-assessed. Many children at Key Stage 1 do not even realise they are taking a test.

Key Stage 2 tests take place in one week in May. All children sit the same test at the same time. In 2004, the tests will take place in the week of **10–14 May**. Your child's school will be able to provide you with a detailed timetable.

Key Stage 3 students will sit their tests on **4–7 May 2004**.

Introduction

Levels

National average levels have been set for children's results in the National Tests. The levels are as follows:

LEVEL	AGE 7 (Key Stage 1)	AGE 11 (Key Stage 2)	AGE 14 (Key Stage 3)
8			
7			
6			
5			
4			
3			
2			
2a			
2b			
2c			
1			

- BELOW EXPECTED LEVEL
- EXPECTED LEVEL
- ABOVE EXPECTED LEVEL
- EXCEPTIONAL

Results

Your child's school will send you a report indicating his or her levels in the tests and the teacher assessment.

The school's overall test results will be included in local and national league tables, which are published in most newspapers.

What can parents do to help?

While it is never a good idea to encourage cramming, you can help your child to succeed by:

- making sure he or she has enough food, sleep and leisure time during the test period;
- practising important skills such as writing and reading stories, spelling and mental arithmetic;
- telling him or her what to expect in the test, such as important symbols and key words;
- helping him or her to be comfortable in test conditions, including working within a time limit, reading questions carefully and understanding different ways of answering.

Introduction

How to use this book

The purposes of this book

- To prepare children for Key Stage 2 National Tests in English by giving them practice, so that they will be familiar with the form of the tests they will take.
- To help parents to judge their children's progress in English.

The practice tests

This book includes practice tests on Reading, Writing and Spelling (Levels 3–5).

Answers and a marking scheme are provided at the end of the book.

The Reading Test (Levels 3–5)

15 minutes are provided for reading the booklet (cut this out). 45 minutes are allowed for answering the questions.

Most children take the Levels 3–5 test. The Reading Test comprises a variety of texts – perhaps non-fiction, fiction and poetry – testing reading strategies across a range of genres. There will normally be a link or a common theme between the passages.

The questions set will require four different kinds of answer:

- short words or phrases. Usually one mark is allocated for each correct response;
- longer answers – one or two sentences. Usually two marks are allocated for these answers as they require more understanding of the text;
- detailed explanations of opinion. These involve a more personal approach. Up to three marks are allocated;
- multiple choice – where several choices are given and the child should choose the correct one. Single marks are allocated for each correct response.

Incorrect answers are given a zero score, and no half marks are awarded.

Although some of the questions will have a 'right answer', all children will express their responses in a different way. When marking the questions, look for the content of what has been written and not just the quality of the writing, grammar, etc.

The Writing Test (Levels 3–5)

At Key Stage 2 children's writing is assessed through two Writing Tasks:

- a longer Writing Task (45 minutes);
- a shorter Writing Task (20 minutes).

Schools will be told what type of writing tasks to set but the topic is up to the teacher, who will take into account the interest and experience of the class. One **Writing Task** will be based on a story (fiction) and the other on information (non-fiction).

Children should be allowed time to plan their writing for both tasks, which they should not do one after the other.

The **Longer Task** is assessed for: **Sentence structure and punctuation** (up to 8 marks), **Text structure and organisation** (up to 8 marks) and **Composition and effect** (up to 12 marks) (Total 28 marks).

Sentence structure and punctuation focuses on the use of variation of types of sentence, clarity, purpose and effect, and on grammatical accuracy and punctuation.

Text structure and organisation focuses on organising and presenting whole texts effectively, sequencing and structuring information, ideas and events, constructing paragraphs and using cohesion within and between paragraphs.

Composition and effect focuses on imaginative, interesting and thoughtful writing, writing a text which is suitable for its purpose and for the reader, and organising and presenting a text effectively.

The **Shorter Task** is assessed for **Sentence structure, punctuation and text organisation** (up to 4 marks) and **Composition and effect** (up to 8 marks) (Total 12 marks).

Spelling is assessed in a separate test (20 marks).

The mark schemes each year are specific to the tests; new level thresholds are set for each year's tests to ensure that standards are maintained each year.

Introduction

The conversion charts to National Curriculum levels provided at the end of this book should be regarded as a rough guide only.

Most children take the Levels 3–5 test.

Children's writing is assessed in two ways:

- purpose and organisation, e.g. if the child is asked to write a letter, has he or she set out the letter correctly? Does he or she show an awareness of the audience of the letter? Has information from the original text been used?

- grammar – style and punctuation, e.g. is the style of the letter correct? What level of sentences is being used? Is the writing clear? Does the use of punctuation help the writer to communicate his or her meaning?

The Spelling Test (Levels 3–5)

10 minutes are allowed for this test.

All children take the Levels 3–5 test. A passage containing gaps is provided. You are provided with the complete passage on page 35 – the words being assessed are in **bold**. Read the passage to your child and pause at each of the twenty missing words to allow him or her time to write the word in the space.

Insights from previous tests

Every year, an analysis of the performance of children in the National Tests is produced. The main points in this analysis can be useful when helping your child to attempt the tests in this book.

Below are some of the recommendations made:

Reading – Encourage your child to:

- look across the text to see any patterns, e.g. a sequence of events, the use of illustrations;
- generalise from two or three instances;
- explain the organisation and layout of texts;
- identify the purpose of the text and the audience for whom it was written;
- explore the precise meaning and effect of words.

Writing – Encourage your child to:

- use commas to mark clauses in longer sentences;
- check the use of commas in lists;
- revise the use of possessive apostrophes (e.g. the dog's bone) at all levels;
- pay more attention to the ending of the writing;
- choose carefully when and where to change to a new paragraph;
- organise paragraphs to make and develop points more effectively.

Introduction

Setting the tests

A relaxed approach is best. If you feel anxious, your child will sense this and might not concentrate or perform as well as he or she could.

Work in a quiet place where you and your child will not be distracted.

Before beginning the tests, cut out pages 1 to 6 and staple them together to make a reading booklet. You may also find it useful to cut out page 35 as your guide for the spelling test.

Your child will need a pencil and, if possible, an eraser. If you do not have an eraser, ask your child to cross out any mistakes made.

Provide some extra paper – although some answers need to be completed in the book.

The tests in this book are modelled as closely as possible on the 'real thing' so pupils will not be surprised by the test format. However, parents can help with the pressure of the tests by using the material in this book as a resource for teaching and learning. Do not just sit your child down with a test and tell him or her to 'get on with it'; share the experiences, questions and discussion that arise. Try sitting one yourself!

- Talk about each of the questions and what your child will need to think about for the answer.

- Point out that there are different types of question, e.g. those which give a choice of answers from which one is chosen and ticked, and those which ask for a written answer.

- Choose a comfortable, secure environment in which to do the tests together.

- Mark the work with your child, praising positive points as well as pointing out things which are not correct.

- Look closely at how the incorrect responses can be corrected, what needs to be learned or changed and how this can be done realistically. It is useful to list just two or three things which need to be done or learned before the next test session.

- Stick to the time limits – but do not insist that the entire test paper has to be completed in one go.

- Give immediate feedback.

- Be positive about achievements!

- Tell your child to have a go at answering every question; and to leave any questions he or she cannot answer, and go back to them at the end.

- If you have any questions, ask your child's teacher.

Introduction

Advice to give to your child

- Keep an eye on the time! When you are practising, spend a little longer at first, but aim to become quicker. Remember: you will not be given any extra time in the real test! When your teacher says, 'Put your pens down' – that's it!

- Which question is worth the most marks? Spend more time on that question – but not too much more time.

- Look at how many marks are allocated. Try to make that many points. If there are 2 marks, make 2 points (and back them up with proof). This will keep you looking for information and writing until the end.

- Don't ignore the help you are given on the paper. The questions tell you what to think about. Use these prompts as a plan for your own reading and writing.

- Underline or highlight the key points. You can write on the test papers and it is helpful to do so. You have 15 minutes of reading time to start so you can begin to get ideas and remember where key points are to be found.

- Make your notes before you start to write. The aim is not to fill in as many sheets in your answer book as possible. You only get the one chance so think about what you want to write before you put your pen to paper.

- When you write your answer, write in sentences – don't just copy your notes on to the paper.

- Don't be afraid to cross things out and write them again. It is important to be neat but it is more important to say what you really mean.

- Write in paragraphs (you could leave a line between them) as this makes your work easier to read.

- Use quotations – but not huge chunks! It is best to quote short phrases and single words.

- Good luck!

Reading Test Booklet

Sending a letter

Contents

Introduction 1

Postage Stamps 2
Information

The Wool-Pack 4
Story

The Postman 6
Poem

Introduction

Writing and sending a letter may seem like a very ordinary thing to do, but this was not always the case.

In this booklet we shall look at aspects of sending a letter in three different ways:

- from an information text;
- from a story in which a letter plays an important part;
- from a poem.

You have **15 minutes** to read through these passages.

Postage Stamps

(From *Postage Stamps* by L N and M Williams)

The world's first postage stamps were issued by Great Britain on May 1, 1840, and came into use on May 6. Their introduction was due to the efforts of Rowland Hill, at one time a Birmingham schoolmaster, who produced a plan to reform the Post Office. He succeeded in interesting Parliament in his plan, which was adopted in 1839.

Before 1840 the postage on a letter was usually paid by the person who received it, and, as the postal rates were very high, some people, especially the very poor, used to dread a visit from the postman. Postage was charged according to weight: a letter weighing two ounces (about 55 grammes) sent from London to Croydon cost two shillings and six pence (twelve and a half new pence).

The high charges were caused by inefficient working of the Post Office, and Rowland Hill's plan showed that letters could be sent all over the country for one old penny each (less than one penny today), and still enable the Post Office to make a good profit. So as to make the sender of a letter responsible for the postage, Hill suggested that it should be paid in advance, by sticking a stamp to a letter.

There were two values of stamps: 1d (one old penny) and 2d, both showing the head of Queen Victoria. They were printed in London in sheets of 240 stamps, and were 'imperforate' (having no perforations). Although over 150 years old the Penny Black and the Twopenny Blue are not very rare, but are in great demand by collectors.

Two years after Britain had introduced postage stamps to the world, a private postal service, working in New York, issued a stamp, the first to appear in the Western Hemisphere. Other issues by postmasters in the United States were made in the next few years and in 1847 came the first stamps for use throughout the USA, with two values: Five Cents Brown, showing Benjamin Franklin, and Ten Cents Black, showing George Washington.

In the meantime, the Swiss canton of Zurich brought out two stamps, four and six 'rappen'. Then from Geneva came a curious stamp: it was in two halves. If one wanted to post a double weight letter the whole stamp had to be used, but for an ordinary letter the stamp was cut in two and one half affixed. This stamp is known to collectors as 'The Double Geneva'. A picturesque issue from Basle (also spelt Basel), in July 1845, showed a dove in flight. Known as the 'Basle Dove', this was the first multi-coloured stamp, the dove being embossed in white on a red background with pale blue corners.

The Wool-Pack
by Cynthia Harnett

Nicholas Fetterlock is the son of a fifteenth-century wool merchant. He is fourteen and has an arranged marriage with Cecily – an eleven-year-old. He needs to write her a letter.

For hours Nicholas sat in misery at his father's counter, scratching his nose with the end of his quill. When he appealed to Master Richard for help, the priest replied with a smile that love letters were outside his province, and Nicholas should follow the guidance of his heart. But Nicholas' heart offered no suggestions. At last, in despair, he submitted to his mother's control, and wrote at her dictation a letter based on a scribe's collection of model letters. It was full of fine phrases and began by addressing Cecily as 'Worshipful mistress and most sweet cousin' ('cousin', he was told, being a useful term which would cover any tie). It commended her piously to the care of the blessed saints, told her that he took no pleasure in life until he might be with her again, and that he was her true lover and humble servant.

He grinned to himself as he scattered sand on the ink, remembering Cecily up a tree, Cecily running away to track the Lombards, Cecily stamping her foot at them at the Fair. He sealed the letter with his father's seal – the merchant's mark so despised by Mistress Fetterlock – and then tried to forget it as quickly as possible.

The reply came in less than a fortnight, written in a round, childish hand. He had not known for certain that Cecily could write. After all, many girls were not taught anything but the domestic arts. But flowery as the letter was, he recognised a touch of the real Cecily about it. She called Nicholas her 'well-beloved Valentine' and told him that if only he were satisfied with her she would be 'the merriest maiden alive'. He laughed out loud at that.

But he had not finished with his letter-writing. One evening Giles took him aside.

'You are a scholar, young master,' he began. 'Could you make a letter for me to your worshipful father?'

Nicholas stared at him. 'Has anything happened that is new?' he cried.

Giles shook his head. 'It is just that Leach is sending away the wool for Calais. I have discovered reason after reason why it should not go, hoping that the master would come back. But now Leach will wait no longer. He is the packer and I cannot stop him. But I shall sleep better o' nights when your father has been told. I am no scholar, Master Nicholas, and I would not trust this matter to a scribe.'

That was true. It would never do to bring a public letter-writer to do it.

'I could write the letter,' said Nicholas. 'But how could we send it? My mother's messenger left yesterday. There will not be another for a week.'

'I have thought of that,' replied the shepherd. 'There is a man who rides regularly for the Abbot of Gloucester. He is courting my niece, and he will surely call at the barber's tomorrow on his way to London.'

Nicholas sighed. There seemed to be no help for it. And if the letter was to go in the morning there was no time to spare.

The Postman

Satchel on hip
the postman goes
from doorstep to doorstep
and stooping sows

each letterbox
with seed. His right
hand all the morning makes
the same half circle. White

seed he scatters,
a fistful of
featureless letters
pregnant with ruin or love.

I watch him zig-
zag down the street
dipping his hand in that big
bag, sowing the cool, neat

envelopes which
make *twenty-one*
unaccountably rich,
twenty-two an orphan.

I cannot see
them but I know
others are watching. We
stoop in a row
(as he turns away),

straighten and stand
weighing and delaying
the future in one hand.

Jon Stallworthy

Reading Test Questions

Sending a letter

On the following pages, there are different types of question for you to answer in different ways. The space for your answer shows you what type of writing is needed.

Short answers
Some questions are followed by one line.
This shows that you need only write a word or a phrase in your answer.

Several line answers
Some questions are followed by two or three lines.
This gives you space to write more words or a sentence or two.

Longer answers
Some questions are followed by more than three lines.
This shows that a longer, more detailed answer is needed to explain your opinion.
You can write in full sentences if you want to.

Multiple choice answers
For these questions you need to do no writing at all.
You need to choose the best word or group of words to fit the passage and put a ring around your choice.

Marks
The number under each circle in the margin tells you the maximum number of marks for each question.

Please wait until you are told to start work on page 8. You should work through the questions until you are asked to stop, referring to your reading booklet when you need to.

You will have **45 minutes** for this test.

Reading Test

These questions are about **Postage Stamps**.

Choose the best number, word or group of words to fit the passage and put a ring around your choice.

1 The world's first postage stamps were issued in

| 1839 | 1840 ✓ | 1845 | 1847 |

2 Before this date, postage was paid by

| the very poor | the sender of a letter | the person who received the letter | the Post Office |

3 Posting a letter was very expensive

| because of inefficient working by the Post Office | because there were two values for stamps | because letters were not very heavy | because stamps were 'imperforate' |

4 After Britain, the next place in the world to produce stamps was

| Washington | New York | Geneva | Basle |

5 Below is a summary of events in the history of the postage stamp, but they are mixed up. Number each stage in the correct order.

3	Stamps come into use
1	The British Parliament adopts Rowland Hill's plan to reform the Post Office
2	1d and 2d stamps issued
4	First private postal service in the Western Hemisphere started

TOTAL 5

Reading Test

6 Write down **two things** we learn about Rowland Hill's life from the passage.

~~he left trying~~ but he came from the Birmingham. He was a school teacher and in his parliament plan which was adopted

[2] 2

7 Give one reason why the poor used to dread a visit from the postman before 1840.

Postal the rates were letter very ~~with high~~ expensive

[1] 1

8 Explain **two ways** in which Rowland Hill made a difference to the way that postage was paid.

Stamps were ~~mam~~ introduced

The sender paid the postage.

[2] 2

5

TOTAL

3

5

Reading Test

9 Draw lines to match the stamps to their place of origin.

Twopenny Blue		Basle
Ten Cents Black		Zurich
Four and six 'rappen' stamps		USA
A multicoloured stamp		Britain

10 Explain what was curious about 'The Double Geneva'.

if you sent an ordinary letter they cut it in two.

11 What was the purpose of designing the stamp in this way?

so they didn't have to use as much paper.

12 Label this diagram to show that this stamp is a 'Basle Dove'.

— Dove (white)
— Red background
— pale blue corner

TOTAL 8

Reading Test

These questions are about the passage from **The Wool-Pack**.

13 Complete the chart with information from the passage about writing and sending letters.

Today	In the fifteenth century
We write with a pen	People wrote with a quill
our ink drys fast	People used sand to dry the ink
Letters can take a day to be delivered	Letters could take more than a week
We put letters in envelopes	they sealed the paper
Letters are delivered by a postman	Letters were delivered by a messenger.

2 / 2

14 Give two examples of language which show that the book was written about a time long ago.

'The merriest maiden alive' and 'you are a scholar young master'.

1 / 2

15 Explain why and how Nicholas 'submitted to his mother's control, and wrote at her dictation'.

he wrote what his mom told him to because he couldn't think of anything to write.

3 / 3

TOTAL 6 / 7

Reading Test

16 After he had finished the letter, why do you think Nicholas grinned to himself when he thought about Cecily?

because he was writing a very important letter and he remembered about cicily doing funny things

3
3

17 Why was Nicholas surprised to receive a reply from Cecily?

because usually girls couldn't read

0
1

18 What reason does he give for this?

because most girls were only taught the domestic arts.

2
2

19 What reasons does Giles give for not writing a letter? Use your own words.

he said he is not a scholar so he couldnt write very well or at all.

3
3

TOTAL

8
9

These questions are about the poem **The Postman**.

20 Where does the postman go to in the first verses of the poem?

The postman goes from doorstep to doorstep.

21 What is he actually doing?

The postman is delivering the post

22 The poet describes him as someone who 'sows'. What kind of person normally sows?

~~Firmer~~ farmer

23 To what does the poet compare the letters in the second verse of the poem?

seed.

24 Why are the letters 'featureless'?

envelopes have basicly nothing on them so it is pretty much boring

25 Why does the writer describe the postman as zig-zagging down the street?

because he moves from house to house in a zig zagy ~~~~ pattern.

Reading Test

26 'envelopes which
make *twenty-one*
unaccountably rich,
twenty-two an orphan.'

Why are the words 'twenty-one' and 'twenty-two' printed in italics?

because 21 and 22 are numbers of the houses he goes to.

3 / 3

27 Find three words in the poem which describe the movement of the postman as he does his job. Write one word next to each dot.

- stooping
- dipping
- sowing

3 / 3

28 Explain why the people in the house are

'weighing and delaying
the future in one hand'

when they pick up their letters.

because they don't know what type of story is in it so they are trying to figure it out.

3 / 3

TOTAL 9 / 9

Reading Test

These questions are about all three texts **Sending a letter**.

29 The three texts were written by different people for different audiences.

Match the text to the audience with a line.
Draw one line to each box.

Text		Audience
Postage Stamps	╲	Someone who is interested in making an imaginative picture about an everyday occurrence.
The Wool-Pack	╳	Someone interested in history who wants information.
The Postman	╱	Someone interested in the past who wants to imagine how people would have behaved.

3

TOTAL

3

15

Reading Test

30 Some readers may not think that sending a letter is anything out of the ordinary.

Explain why these three passages might change their view.

because the first one tells you about history of post stamps how they developed and came into use. The other one is about how sending letters a long time ago. and the last one tells you a different view of a postman or postwoman.

Assesed and malked By Camille R-Grant Rianna

53 / 57

3

TOTAL
3
3

Writing Test: Information

Instructions

Choose **one** piece of writing from the following:

1. *I felt I must write…* (a letter to persuade); **or**

2. *Number On Window Catches Thieves* (a newspaper article).

Someone is allowed to read through this section with you.

Plan and organise your ideas in the spaces provided.

Spend about 15 minutes thinking about what to write and making a note of your ideas.

You will have a total of **45 minutes**.

Writing Test

I felt I must write…

You read this letter in your local newspaper. You are so angry about what it says that you decide to write a letter opposing this view.

Write your letter. The purpose is to persuade people that the letter writer's view is wrong.

> I don't know what's wrong with the young people of today. All this moaning about bullying in schools. When I was a child it was never bullying just because someone called you a few names or hit you once or twice.
>
> Everyone in school gets picked on for some reason but you have to be strong enough to fight back. If you can't fight back then you must be a weed, that's all I can say.
>
> My child came home the other day with a letter from his teacher saying they have to talk about what is happening to them and that they have to tell teachers. This is just telling kids to tell on their mates.

You should think about:

- how you will start the letter;
- the best way to organise your arguments;
- how to make the points as clearly as possible;
- how to finish your letter.

Remember:

- you are trying to persuade someone to share your views.

You can make notes in this space.

Writing Test

Number On Window Catches Thieves

What story might this newspaper headline be describing?

Imagine you are a newspaper reporter who has to write about the event.

Write an article about what happened. Make it as exciting as possible.

You should think about:

- the sort of information you need to include;
- how you will start the newspaper report;
- the best way to organise your points;
- how to make the points as clearly as possible;
- how to finish your article.

Remember:

- you are giving people information as well as making it exciting for your reader.

You can make notes on page 19.

Writing Test: Story

Instructions

Choose **one** piece of writing from the following:

1. *A Day in _____ Street* (a description or short story); **or**

2. *The Letter* (a short story).

Someone is allowed to read through this section with you.

Plan and organise your ideas in the space provided.

Spend about 5 minutes thinking about what to write and making a note of your ideas.

You will have a total of **20 minutes**.

A Day in _____ Street

Make up a name for the street. Decide what kind of street it is. Imagine the events of a day in the street.

You should think about:

- buildings and other objects;
- people;
- what happens.

Questions to ask yourself:

- What are the characters like?
- How can I show this in a very short story?
- What are the relationships between the characters?

You can make notes in this space.

The Letter

Imagine that you find this fragment of a letter. Tell the story of what happens and how you explain the mystery.

> Go to the tower
>   You will see
> Beware of the door on the left. It has a magic
>
> Remember what you have learned at school about the power of the owls.

You should think about:

- how you found the letter;
- what happened;
- who was involved;
- how the mystery was solved.

Remember:

- characters;
- the setting;
- how you will begin the story or description;
- what happens;
- how you will end the piece.

You can make notes on page 24.

Writing Test

As I entered traparr Street I saw people Smacking each other with thier slippers I entered the magic door I saw this lady and this this man after few years they became my nanny and grandad. But when they came to my house.

Spelling Test

The first stamps were ___issued___ in May 1840. Rowland Hill produced a plan to change the Post Office and he ___succeeded___ in persuading Parliament that this was a good ___plan___.

Before this time, postage was _____ paid by the person who _____ the letter – a very different situation from today. The cost of postage was very _____ because it was determined by _____ and _____ to the _____ that it had to _____. This meant that the very poor used to dread a visit from the postman, _____ if the letter had come from afar.

The Post Office was also very _____, which led to high charges. Rowland Hill _____ that letters could be delivered all over the _____ for only one penny each.

In order to do this, the sender had to be _____ for the cost of the postage, so _____ people being charged for letters which they did not expect.

The first stamps – a Penny Black and a Twopenny Blue – are now much looked for by _____. In the second half of the nineteenth century, all over the world, postal services began to grow, _____ about by the work of Rowland Hill in Britain. _____ his example we now have many _____ stamps – including a triangular-shaped one from South Africa and a two-part one from Switzerland.

TOTAL
20

25

Answers
Reading Test

POSTAGE STAMPS (Information)

1 The world's first postage stamps were issued in 1840.   **1 mark**

2 Before this date, postage was paid by the person who received the letter.   **1 mark**

3 Posting a letter was very expensive because of inefficient working by the Post Office.   **1 mark**

4 After Britain, the next place in the world to produce stamps was New York.   **1 mark**

5   **1 mark**

3	Stamps come into use
1	The British Parliament adopts Rowland Hill's plan to reform the Post Office
2	Id and 2d stamps issued
4	First private postal service in the Western Hemisphere started

6 He came from Birmingham; he was a schoolteacher.   **2 marks**

7 **One** of the following:
Postal rates were very high.
Postal rates were paid by the person who received the post.
The poor could not afford to receive post.   **1 mark**

8 Any **two** from:
All post in Britain cost one penny (1d) or 2d.
The sender paid the postage.
The postage was paid for in advance.
Stamps were introduced.   **2 marks**

9   **2 marks**

Twopenny Blue	Britain
Ten Cents Black	USA
Four and six 'rappen' stamps	Zurich
A multicoloured stamp	Basle

10 This stamp was made in two separate halves.   **1 mark**

Answers

11 It would be more versatile. Double weight letters took both parts of the stamp. Ordinary weight letters took one half. **2 marks**

12 Parts that could be labelled are:
a flying dove
red background
corners (in blue in the original) **3 marks**

Maximum mark: 18

THE WOOL-PACK (Story)

13 **2 marks**

Today	In the fifteenth century
We write with a pen	People wrote with a quill
We use blotting paper or quick-drying ink	People used sand to dry the ink
Letters can take a day to be delivered	Letters took weeks
We put letters in envelopes	People used seals and sealing wax
Letters are delivered by a postman	Letters were delivered by messenger

14 Examples could include:
People's titles – 'scribe', 'mistress', 'maiden'.
Expressions of speech and writing – 'worshipful mistress'.
Subject matter of the story – the wool trade.
Different ways of doing things, e.g. the shepherd, scribes to write letters, distances to cover. **2 marks**

15 He could not think of anything to write himself.
He allowed his mother to tell him what to write.
He copied down what she said to him. **3 marks**

16 The letter he had just written was very serious but he remembered her acting as a child, e.g. climbing a tree and stamping her foot. **3 marks**

17 He did not know for certain that she could write. **1 mark**

Answers

18 Many girls at the time were not taught to read or write. They were taught to perform household tasks – 'domestic arts'. **2 marks**

19 Giles is 'no scholar' – he probably could not read or write.
He would not trust the secret content of the letter to a 'public scribe' – someone who wrote letters as a job and who might tell others about what the letter contained. **3 marks**

Maximum mark: 16

THE POSTMAN (Poem)

20 He moves from doorstep to doorstep – from house to house. **1 mark**

21 He is delivering letters – moving from house to house to post the letters through the houses' letter-boxes. **1 mark**

22 A farmer **1 mark**

23 Seeds **1 mark**

24 Often the outsides of letters tell you nothing about what is inside them.
Envelopes are often plain. **2 marks**

25 He is moving to and fro across the street in an irregular line. **2 marks**

26 These are the numbers of the houses which he visits.
The italics tell us what might be written on the envelopes he is holding. **3 marks**

27 Any **three** from:
Goes   Scatters
Stooping   Dipping
Zig-zag   Sowing
Turns away
3 marks

28 The letters may contain news which is good or bad. This could change people's lives. The people don't know what is in the letters before they open them but they pause and think about it as they pick them up. **3 marks**

Maximum mark: 17

Answers

GENERAL

29 The boxes should be matched as follows: **3 marks**

Text	Audience
Postage Stamps	Someone interested in history who wants information.
The Wool-Pack	Someone interested in the past who wants to imagine how people would have behaved.
The Postman	Someone who is interested in making an imaginative picture about an everyday occurrence.

30 The factual, information passage tells you why and how postage stamps developed.
The story tells us how different it was sending a letter five hundred years ago.
The poem gives us an unusual view of an 'ordinary' postman. **3 marks**

Maximum mark: 6

Answers
Writing Test

The **Longer Task** is assessed by looking at **three** things:

Sentence structure and punctuation focuses on the use of variation of types of sentence, clarity, purpose and effect, and on grammatical accuracy and punctuation (up to 8 marks).

Text structure and organisation focuses on organising and presenting whole texts effectively, sequencing and structuring information, ideas and events, constructing paragraphs and using cohesion within and between paragraphs (up to 8 marks).

Composition and effect focuses on imaginative, interesting and thoughtful writing, writing a text which is suitable for its purpose and for the reader, and organising and presenting a text effectively (up to 12 marks).

The maximum mark available for this task is 28 marks.

The **Shorter Task** is assessed for **Sentence structure, punctuation and text organisation** (up to 4 marks) and **Composition and effect** (up to 8 marks) (Total 12 marks).

Marking in this way can enable you to see the strengths and weaknesses of your child. After all, we cannot all be good at all areas of English.

On the next few pages are some charts to help you to assess your child's writing. It is not an 'exact science'. Look at the description that best fits the overall performance of your child and allocate the marks given for that level.

Answers

Longer Task (Information)	
Sentence structure and punctuation (maximum mark: 8)	**Marks**
Joins parts of sentences mostly with *and* and *but*. Uses some simple sentences, often brief, with modal verbs to indicate what ought to happen (for example, *we should treat all name calling as bullying*). Sometimes demarcates sentences with capital letters and full stops.	1
Uses a limited range of time connectives: *and* and *then* to link clauses: (for example, *The thieves broke the window and lifted the latch, then they climbed in*). Subjects and verbs are frequently repeated. Use of modal verbs: for example, *children should always report bullying*. Noun phrases mostly simple (for example, *a number*) with occasional expansion (for example, *stocking masks*). Sometimes includes generalising words: for example, *every, only*. Uses full stops, capital letters, exclamation marks and question marks to demarcate sentences, mostly accurately; uses commas in lists.	2–3
Develops explanation within sentences through using subordinating connectives (*if, because*): for example, *because it would make a bully think twice before saying or doing anything to harm anyone*. Varies the construction of sentences using adverbials (for example, *at the end of the day*) and expanded noun phrases (for example, *the clever young police constable*). Verbs refer to possible events (for example, *it would be a good idea to…*), future time (for example, *we shall make a note of any bullying*) and sometimes the present (for example, *I hope*). There is some correct use of commas within sentences to mark phrases or clauses.	4–5
Verbs are varied and express a range of time reference: for example, *we have been discussing; we expect to hear*. Uses simple and complex sentences, with some variety of connectives: for example, the subordinating conjunctions *which* and *who* (*the detective who solved the case*). Uses expanded phrases and clauses to express ideas economically (*counsellors to help anyone who is bullied*). Qualifying words and phrases (*a little better, too much, very brave*) contribute to precision. Almost all sentences are correctly demarcated with a range of punctuation: for example, brackets, dashes and colons.	6–7
Varies the lengths and focuses of sentences to express shades of meaning: for example, might use passives (*would be given help by the pupil-counsellors*). Word order may be manipulated for emphasis: for example, *lastly, and most importantly*. Sentences may include embedded subordinate clauses for economy of expression: for example, *most bullies, as has already been mentioned, are cowards*. Uses a range of punctuation correctly (full stops, commas, colons, semi-colons, question marks, exclamation marks and dashes), with little omission, to mark the structure of sentences and texts and to give clarity.	8

Text structure and organisation (maximum mark: 8)	**Marks**
Groups ideas into sequences of sentences, with some division possibly indicated by layout: for example, line breaks or boxes might be used. The organisation of the argument might be chronological rather than logical. Uses simple connectives (*and, but*). There is some connection between sentences: for example, through the use of pronouns referring to the same thing (*he, she, it, they, that boy, those houses*).	1

Answers

Text structure and organisation (continued)	Marks
Simple overall text structure includes brief introduction or concluding statement: for example, *that's what I think should be done*. Indicates some divisions between sections of the content: sub-headings, use of *also* for additional information (*there are also*) and paragraphs. Relationships between ideas in the argument are usually non-chronological, similar ideas usually being grouped together. Uses pronouns to make connections between sentences, by referring to people or things in the previous sentence: for example, *he, she, it, they, their*.	2–3
The structure of the text includes an introduction, logically ordered points and a conclusion. Consistently indicates new sections by new paragraphs; uses introductory phrases (and sub-headings, where appropriate). If used, conventional phrases are integrated into the text (*the first point, the second point, the last point*).	4–5
Relationships between paragraphs give a structure to the whole text: for example, connections make the structure clear to the reader by referring forwards and backwards: for example, *after doing this, what it should mean is*. Develops paragraphs: supports main ideas consistently with relevant arguments or details.	6–7
Sequencing of sections contributes to overall effectiveness of text: for example, by placing the most interesting or appealing idea to give maximum impact. The news article might begin with a sentence, or even a paragraph, which attracts attention before going on to report the facts. Varies the length and structure of paragraphs, giving each paragraph a clear focus, and organising the content by reference within and between paragraphs.	8

Composition and effect (maximum mark: 12)	Marks
Writes a short series of points and comments about the topic; their purpose might not be clear. There is some attempt to interest the reader: for example, by using examples or quotations.	1–2
In the letter, uses persuasive words and phrases: for example, *no one could possibly disagree, moreover, surely*. In the newspaper report, indicates shifts of time through the use of time connectives: for example, *three days earlier, afterwards, the next morning*. The writing shows evidence of a viewpoint. There is evidence that the writer has tried to write in a specific style: formal or informal, as appropriate to the reader and context.	3–5
Adapts the persuasive or narrative form to the situation: for example, the content is informative; the details are well placed to present a clear argument and it appeals to the reader by being eye-catching: for example, through the use of a headline and sub-headings. The writer's viewpoint is established and maintained: for example, the writing suggests the writer's concern or amusement, as appropriate.	6–8
Adapts ideas to suit the intended reader. Establishes and controls a clear and consistent viewpoint, with the form of address consistently either formal or informal, as appropriate for the reader and context. Maintains the reader's interest through the use of stylistic devices: for example, synonyms to avoid repetition (*soon/before long, huge/massive/vast, hardly anyone/scarcely anyone/few people*). Interesting use of or unusual vocabulary directs the reader's attention to the main idea.	9–11
The writer's choice of content and the way in which it is arranged are suited to the intended reader: for example, through comments which are thought to be of interest to the reader (*no child should be bullied, you can do something about it*). The writer's viewpoint is well expressed and convincing.	12

Maximum mark: 28

Answers

Shorter Task (Story)	
Sentence structure, punctuation and text organisation (maximum mark: 4)	**Marks**
Uses some simple sentences, mainly simple grammatically accurate statements in the past tense. Usually starts with the third person: for example, *they peered through the hole*. Uses capital letters to begin most sentences and full stops to end them. Clauses are usually grammatically accurate, mostly joined with *and*, *but* and *then*. May use simple repetition for emphasis: for example, *a long, long way*, *very very big*. Makes some connections between sentences: for example, through the use of pronouns referring back to people or things (*it*, *they*).	1
Uses the first or third person and the past tense consistently. Writes mostly compound sentences, with clauses linked by connectives: for example, *and*, *but* and *so*. Uses simple adjectives: for example, *big, good, small*. Uses full stops and capital letters accurately. Might use commas in lists. Uses apostrophes accurately. Uses simple adjectives: for example, *good, long, wide, old*. Often repeats subjects and verbs (*it had*, *it was*). Clauses are mostly joined with *and*, *but* and *or*, with some use of *if*. Expands some sentences with simple adverbials: for example, *slowly, upwards*. Sometimes makes explicit the relationships between sentences or clauses: for example, through giving additional information.	2
Uses grammatically accurate clauses. Uses some imaginative adjectives: for example, *skilful, talented*. Might use comparative or superlative adjectives: for example, *better, best, neater, neatest*. Varies the sentence construction: for example, adverbials (*in the street, over the wall*) and expanded noun phrases (*a shrill scream, a low whisper*) to describe activity or indicate the writer's attitude to an experience (*he had the cheek to say…*). Varies verbs for time reference: for example, modals (*he was fuming with anger; they might have heard him*). Uses prepositions for spatial description (*through the doors, over the wall*). Uses some subordinating connectives: for example, *if* and *when*. Some commas mark phrases or clauses.	3
Varies the sentence lengths. Qualifies adjectives with adverbs: for example, *fairly, quite, very*. Uses some of the more sophisticated punctuation marks where appropriate: semi-colons, colons, dashes, ellipses. Uses compound and complex sentences with varied connectives: for example, *which* and *although*, and varied sentence constructions for effect: for example, using passives to alter the focus of attention and short sentences for emphasis.	4

Composition and effect (maximum mark: 8)	**Marks**
Groups some of the ideas into sets of sentences. Sometimes the layout splits ideas into groups: for example, starting on a new line, writing in a box, using a sub-heading.	1
Includes a range of relevant details, in which some parts are grouped by topic, but these groupings might not be consistent. Indicates some divisions between sections of the content: for example, by using headings, line breaks or paragraphing.	2–3
Introduces an opinion or point of view (but might not maintain it): for example, description in the third person.	4–5
Maintains a point of view (for example, description in the third person) for most of the writing.	6–7
Maintains a point of view (for example, description in the third person) throughout the text. Tailors the text to the reader (for example, through the use of appropriate vocabulary). The voice of the writer is well expressed and convincing: for example, the writer adopts a persona whose character becomes apparent as the account of the experience unfolds. Manipulates stylistic devices to support the purpose fully and to entertain the audience: for example, figurative language such as comparisons, similes and metaphors.	8

Maximum mark: 12

Answers

The words missing from your child's spelling test are those printed in bold below. Read the passage to your child, then read it again, pausing at the words in bold to allow your child to write the missing word in the text. Give one mark for each correct answer.

Maximum mark: 20

The first stamps were **issued** in May 1840. Rowland Hill produced a plan to change the Post Office and he **succeeded** in persuading Parliament that this was a good **idea**.

Before this time, postage was **usually** paid by the person who **received** the letter – a very different situation from today. The cost of postage was very **high** because it was determined by **weight** and **according** to the **distance** that it had to **travel**. This meant that the very poor used to dread a visit from the postman, **especially** if the letter had come from afar.

The Post Office was also very **inefficient**, which led to high charges. Rowland Hill **showed** that letters could be delivered all over the **country** for only one penny each.

In order to do this, the sender had to be **responsible** for the cost of the postage, so **stopping** people being charged for letters which they did not expect.

The first stamps – a Penny Black and a Twopenny Blue – are now much looked for by **collectors**. In the second half of the nineteenth century, all over the world, postal services began to grow, **brought** about by the work of Rowland Hill in Britain. **Through** his example we now have many **curious** stamps – including a triangular-shaped one from South Africa and a two-part one from Switzerland.

National Curriculum Levels

Use the conversion tables below to gain an idea of your child's National Curriculum level from his or her test marks.

Reading

Mark	Level	Mark	Level
Information Reading		**Fiction Reading**	
0–4	Below Level 2	0–1	Below Level 2
5–8	Level 2	2–5	Level 2
9–12	Level 3	6–9	Level 3
13–15	Level 4	10–13	Level 4
16–18	Level 5	14–16	Level 5
Poetry Reading		**General**	
0–1	Below Level 2	0	Below Level 2
2–5	Level 2	1–2	Level 2
6–9	Level 3	3–4	Level 3
10–13	Level 4	5	Level 4
14–17	Level 5	6	Level 5

Spelling

Mark	Level
0–3	Below Level 3
4–9	Level 3
10–14	Level 4
15–20	Level 5

Writing and Spelling

Write your child's marks here:

Writing: Longer Task	
Writing: Shorter Task	
Spelling	
Total	

Writing and Spelling: Approximate National Curriculum Levels

Marks	0–15	16–34	35–49	50–60
Level	Below Level 3	3	4	5

If your child needs more practice in any English topics, use the WHSmith Key Stage 2 English Revision Guide.